FACSIMILES

OF

TOMBSTONES, &c.,

CONNECTED WITH

ST. MARY'S CHURCH,

FORT ST. GEORGE,

MADRAS.

———◆———

EXECUTED UNDER THE ORDERS OF

HIS GRACE THE DUKE OF BUCKINGHAM AND
CHANDOS, G.C.S.I., C.I.E.,
GOVERNOR,

By the Revenue Survey Department,
Madras,

1880.

NOTES.

St. Mary's Church was the first Protestant Church erected in India. It was built during the administration of Mr. Streynsham Master, who was Governor from January 1678 to July 1681. The foundations were commenced on Lady Day in the year 1678, and the work was completed in two years and a half. The opening of the Church is noticed in the Consultations as follows :—

"Thursday, 28th October 1680.—The new Church was dedicated by virtue of Commissions directed to the Government, and to Mr. Richard Portman, the minister, from His Lordship the Bishop of London. The solemnity was performed in very good order, and concluded with vollies of small shot fired by the whole garrison drawn out and the cannon round the Fort. The Church named St. Mary's as at first intended and from this day forward all public service to be there performed."

"It is observable that at the dedication of a new Church by the French Padres and Portuguese in 1675, Sir William Langhorne, then Agent, had fired guns from the Fort; and yet at this time neither Padre nor Portuguese appeared at the dedication of our Church, nor so much as gave the Governor a visit afterwards to wish him joy of it."

The expenses of the building were to be entirely defrayed by the voluntary subscriptions of the English residents, but twelve years later the intention of the Honourable Company to present a peal of bells was notified in a General Letter, dated 22nd January 1692, from the Directors to the Agency at Fort Saint George in the following terms :—

"We have desired Captain Goldsborough to go in hand immediately with the building of a steeple to your Church, with the money collected for that purpose, according to dimensions given him; and by our next ship we intend to send you a ring of six tunable Bells to fix in our steeple which the founder tells us cannot be cast at this season of the year."

The first minister appointed to the Church was, as mentioned above, the Reverend Richard Portman. The following is a copy of the form of the Latin certificate on which he was instituted, made from a now nearly illegible draft of the document which is given in Plate 100.

THE CERTIFITE TO BE SUBSCRIBED BY YE COM^r.

Reverendo in Christo Patri et Dno, Dno Henrico pmissione divina London Episcopo, vrove vicario in spualibus generali, et Offili principali Itimè constituto, ejusve surro, aut alii Judici in hac parte competenti cuicumque, vester humilis et devotus Streynshamus Master Armiger Agens pro honorabili societate sive Comitatu Mercatorum Londinensium apud Indos Orientales missus, et Gubernator Castri s^ti Georgii, Com^rius vester in hac parte Itimè authorizatus, omnimodam reverentiam et obedientiam tanto Reverendo Patri debitas et condignas. Lras vras Com^les (pntibus annex:) nup cum ea (qua decuit) reventia humiles recepimus . . . . cujus vigore pariter et authoritate Richardo Portman Clico (28° die Mensis Octobris Anno Dni 1680 coram nobis psonalr comparen:) juramenta allegiantiæ et supremitatis Regiæ Majestatis detulimus, idemque Richardus Portman eodem die in pntia nra Tribus Ar^lis Xis Lris vestris Com^libus annex: manu sua propria subscripsit, ac Pacto sive fœderi solenni renunciavit, et sic Lras vestras Com^les quantum in nobis ft diligenter executi fuimus. In cujus rei testimonium manum et sigillum nrum ad arma pntibus apposuimus. Dat: 28° die mensis Decembris Anno Dni 1680.

THE CERTIFICATE TO BE SUBSCRIBED BY THE COMMISSARY.

Reverendo in Christo Patri et Domino, Domino Henrico, permissione divina London Episcopo, vestrove Vicario in spiritualibus generali, et Officiali principali legitimè constituto, ejusve surrogato, aut alii Judici in hac parte competenti cuicumque, vester humilis et devotus Streynshamus Master Armiger Agens pro

honorabili societate, sive comitatu Mercatorum Londinensium
apud Indos Orientales missus, et Gubernator Castri Sancti Georgii,
Commissarius vester in hac parte legitimè authorizatus, omnimodam Reverentiam et Obedientiam tanto Reverendo Patri debitas
et condignas. Litteras vestras comitiales (præsentibus annexis)
nuper cum ea (qua decuit) Reverentia humiles recepimus . . . .
cujus vigore pariter et authoritate Richardo Portman clerico (28°.
die Mensis Octobris Anno Domini 1680 coram nobis personaliter
comparenti) juramenta allegiantiæ et supremitatis Regiæ Majestatis detulimus, idemque Richardus Portman eodem die in
præsentia nostra Tribus Articulis Christianis Litteris vestris
Comitialibus annexis manu sua propria subscripsit, ac pacto sive
fœderi solenni renunciavit, et sic Litteras vestras Comitiales
quantum in nobis fuit diligenter executi fuimus. In cujus rei
testimonium manum et sigillum nostrum ad arma præsentibus
apposuimus. Datum 28°. die Mensis Decembris Anno Domini
1680.

THE TOMBSTONES (Plates 1 to 91) lie within the
railings that surround the Church. They are principally
laid so as to form a pavement on the north side of the
Church between the gate of the enclosure, the door of
the nave, and that of the vestry. Only one of them
(Plate 90) is fixed on the outer wall of the Church.

They appear to have been removed to the present
site from the cemeteries that formerly existed on the
esplanades without the Fort, where a few monuments still
remain and where the ground is said to be full of graves.
It is, however, probable that the stone in memory of
GOVERNOR FRANCIS HASTINGS (Plate 91) marks the actual
spot of his interment; he was appointed President in
January 1720, but was superseded after holding office
for a year and a half, and died just on the eve of embark-
ation for home. The record in the Consultations is :

" Friday, 15th December 1721. This evening died the late President, Francis Hastings, Esq."

The following extracts from records indicate that the removal of the tablets took place subsequent to, and in consequence of, the second siege of the Fort by the French under COUNT LALLY from 14th December 1758 to 16th February 1759 :—

EXTRACT FROM CONSULTATIONS, MILITARY DEPARTMENT,
dated Fort St. George, 15th March 1759.

Letter from the Engineer, Fort St. George, 12th March 1759.

*   *   *   *   *

But above all I must beg leave to mention that we lately suffered great inconveniences from the tombs at the burying ground ; which being large arched structures, placed in a line almost close to each other, and opening into one another, not only protected the enemy from our shot, but afforded them a cover equally safe against our shells. I therefore hope, Honorable Sir and Sirs, while these circumstances are fresh in every one's memory you will be pleased to give orders for removing this evil.

I am, with the greatest respect,
Honorable Sir and Sirs,
Your most obedient humble servant,
JOHN CALL.

ORDERED that the several repairs recommended by Mr. Call to be made to the fortifications be set about with all expedition and particularly that means be immediately taken for levelling the tombs at the burying ground.

EXTRACT FROM CONSULTATIONS, PUBLIC DEPARTMENT,
dated Fort St. George, 29th January 1760.

Letter from the Ministers and Church Wardens of St. Mary's Church, dated the 25th January, read as entered hereafter, setting forth that as it has been found necessary to demolish the tombs and walls of the burying ground in order to extend the esplanade to the northward of the town the Vestry have directed them to request the Board will grant another piece of ground to be appropriated to that use.

ORDERED that the Engineer do pitch upon a proper spot for that purpose.

EXTRACT FROM MINUTES OF THE VESTRY OF ST. MARY'S PARISH, dated Fort St. George, 6th January 1760.

The tombs of the burying ground having been demolished in order to extend the esplanade to the northward of the town, agreed that application be made to the President and Council for the grant of another piece of ground to be appropriated to that use.

IDEM, dated 15th January 1760.

The Church Wardens also acquaint the Vestry that having, pursuant to a Resolution of the 8th January, made application to the Governor and Council for a piece of ground for a burying place, they were acquainted that orders had been given to the Engineer to appoint a spot for that purpose.

The mausoleum on the Light House Esplanade is the only one of the ' arched structures ' now standing. When the others were razed it may possibly have been spared on account of the two memorials it contains being connected so intimately with the Council.

The subject of the first tablet (Plate 92) has a distinct official record in the Consultations dated Thursday, 26th January 1688.

" The Council did not meet this day, the President's only son dying last night, was interred this morning to their great grief and sorrow."

Mr. ELIHU YALE was Governor from 1687 to 1692.

The other tablet (Plate 93) facing it records a vacancy in the Council Chamber; Mr. JOSEPH HYMNERS had been a Member of Council since 1670, and held also the post of Mint Master for several years.

The following petition is of interest as regards the old cemetery.

" To The Honourable William Frazer, Esq., &c.

" The petition of the Ministers and Churchwardens of the Parish of St. Mary's in Fort St. George.

" Humbly representeth—

That whereas the monuments of the dead, and the ground where they are interred are held by most people in some measure sacred, and not lightly applied to any common or profane use, yet it is our misfortune that the English burying place in Fort St. George (where so many of our relations, friends and acquaintants lie buried) is not kept in that decent and due manner it ought to be, but every day profaned and applied to the most vile and undecent uses; for since the year 1701, when an old building that stood in the burying place (and in which the Buffaloes used to be shut) was taken down to build lodgings for the soldiers at the Gate adjoining, the Tombs have been made use of for stables for the Buffaloes; which is not only a thing very undecent, but also a very great damage to those buildings, by having so many stakes drove into the pavement and with the walls to fasten the Buffaloes to.

" Another occasion of our complaint on this subject is the Cocoanut trees standing in the burying place; the profit arising from them, we know is inconsiderable, but the nuisance accruing to the place thereby, we are sure is very great. For the Toddy men have people employed there all the day and almost all the night in drawing and selling of Toddy, so that we are obliged on their account to keep the Gates always open, both by day and by night. And there about eight o'clock at night after work is done is such a resort of basket makers, Scavengers people that look after the Buffaloes and other parriars to drink Toddy, that all the Punch houses in Madras have not half the noise in them; and by reason of the gates lying open, beggars and other vagabonds (who know not where to go) make use of the Tombs to lie in, and what unclean uses the neighbours thereabout do make of that place we forbear to tell. We hope what is here urged together with the reflection it must cast on our Church and nation to have so little regard to the repositories of our dead when all other nations who live among us have so just a regard to theirs will prevail with your Honour, &c., to take this matter into your consideration and to find out some meathod to redress these abuses. And your petitioners as in duty bound shall, &c.

GEORGE LEWIS.
ROBERT JONES. } *Ministers.*
EDWARD BARKHAM. } *Church Wardens.*"
FRANCIS COOKE.

FORT SAINT GEORGE, }
February 19th, 1710. }

Most of the foregoing extracts from Public Records are given in Talboys Wheeler's " Madras in the Olden Time."

THE CHURCH PLATE exhibited in Plates 94 to 98 is of considerable interest.

Plate 94 represents a large silver gilt dish or basin presented to the Church by Governor Yale in 1687. This basin is 17 inches in diameter and weighs 3 lb. 2 oz.

Plates 95 to 98 represent another larger basin and a flagon, also silver gilt, purchased for the use of the Church with the proceeds of a legacy left by Lady Goldsbrough, wife of Sir John Goldsbrough, Commissary General. Sir John died in November 1693, and his wife just five years later. The basin is 23 inches in diameter and weighs 6 lb. 10 oz. The flagon is 10¼ inches in height, its diameter at the top and bottom 7 and 5 inches respectively, and its weight is 2½ lb.

These pieces of plate are still in use.

THE PRAYER for the Honourable East India Company (Plate 99) was issued by the authority of the Bishop of London (Henry Compton), the Company's territories being under the jurisdiction of that See in matters ecclesiastical till 1814, when Thomas Fanshaw Middleton was appointed first Bishop of Calcutta.

This special prayer was used for the Honourable Company till 1849, when it was set aside by Bishop Wilson of Calcutta in favor of the modified form of the Prayer for Parliament as now used in India.

The Plates 1 to 98 of this collection are photolithographs of *facsimile* drawings done by Mr. Thomas Perreire, at the cost of His Grace the Duke of Buckingham and Chandos. The whole work was executed under the supervision of Major C. C. Sargeaunt and J. H. Merriman, Esq., of the Revenue Survey Department.

INDEX NOMINUM.

Name.	Date.	Plate No.
Aislabie, John	...	83
Armenus, Isaac	1734	9
Atkinson, Robert	1711	80
Atkinson, Charles	1714	80
Aubone, Thomas	1725	34
Baker, Elizabeth	1652	86
Barker, John (also his children and grandchildren).	1707	47
Barry, Stephen	1719	42
Bett, Francis	1701	64
Boone, Jane	1710	58
Brabour, John and Deborah	...	66
Brooks, Edward	1722	65
Brooke, William	1700-1	62
Brown, Samuel	1695	44
Brown, Samuel	1698	44
Brown, Richard	1690-1	87
Burniston, Carolina	1708	83
Carvalho, John	1733	12
Casamayor, Noah	1746	46
Chardin, Daniel	1709	58
Clarke, Thomas	1683	11
Cooke, Francis	1711-12	89
Cotterell, John	1724	77
Cornish, John	1664	76
Coyle, Antonius	1725	10
Cradock, Thomas	1712	84
Crawford, Henry	1741	41
DeTorres, Peter	1694	2
Ellis, Francis	1703-4	73
English, Richard	1729	43
Fleetwood, Edward	1711-12	20
Fleetwood, Margaret	1712	20
Foquet, Ann	1715	44
Ford, Edmund	1711	37
Fowke, Anne	1734	16
Fowke, Randall	1745	16

Name.					Date.	Plate No.
Foxcroft, Nathaniel ...	...	...	...	...	1670	85
Fullagar, John ...	...	...	...	...	1727	38
Fullerton, Alexander	...	...	...	...	1723	52
Goulding, John ...	...	...	...	...	1738	14
Gray, Thomas ...	...	...	...	...	1692	3
Greenhill, Henry ...	...	...	...	...	1658	90
Griffin, Mary ...	...	...	...	...	1720	49
Griffin, William ...	...	...	...	...	1722	49
Hastings, Francis ...	...	...	...	...	...	91
Heaton, Samuel ...	...	...	...	...	1708	81
Heaton, Jane ...	...	...	...	...	1701	81
Henriques, Maria ...	...	..	...	...	1684	15
Higginson, Richards	...	...	...	...	1726	54
Hopkins, Charles ...	...	...	...	...	1739	33
Hymners, Joseph ...	...	...	...	...	1680	93
Inscription, English	...	...	...	...	1718-19	53
Do. Armenian	...	...	...	...	1730	1
Do. Tamil	...	...	...	...	1691	13
Jennings, Elizabeth	...	...	...	...	1718-19	39
King, Robert ...	...	...	...	...	1723	22
Lawrance, John ...	...	...	...	...	1720-1	37
Large, Peter ...	...	...	...	...	1694	48
Legg, Hannah ...	...	...	...	...	1717	29
Lister, Joseph ...	...	...	...	...	1706-7	72
Long, Charles ...	...	...	...	...	1720	44
Maubert, John ...	...	...	...	...	1721	36
Marshall ...	...	...	...	...	1701	79
Melicque, Francisca	...	...	...	...	1720	4
Meverell, Ann ...	...	...	...	...	1689	70
Michell, Edward ...	...	...	...	...	1741	28
Midon, Bernardus ...	...	...	...	...	1689	18
Muriell, Lucy ...	...	...	...	...	1755	82
Murray, David ...	...	...	...	...	1732	51
Oadham ...	...	...	...	...	1722-23	43
Oadham, Mathew ...	...	...	...	...	1725	43
Oates, Titus ...	...	...	...	...	1723	55

Name.					Date.	Plate No.
Parao, Narciza Ignacia	...	...	...	...	1742	6
Parham, Mary	...	...	...	...	1700-1	68
Pearson, Battson	...	...	...	...	1697	67
Plumb, Thomas	...	...	...	...	1711-12	19
Plumb, Violante	...	...	...	...	1713-14	19
Plumb, Ann	...	...	...	...	1739	41
Porier, Gabriel	...	...	...	...	1716	17
Porier, Lucy	...	...	...	...	1712	17
Pye, Eleanor	...	...	...	...	1743	50
Ribeira, Domingas	...	...	...	...	1719	7
Robson, Thomas	...	...	...	...	1720	27
Robson, Christopher	...	...	...	...	1719	27
Rushlate, Francis	...	...	...	...	1729-30	24
Saban, Peter Luder	...	...	...	...	1719	35
Scattergood, John	...	...	...	...	...	83
Seaton, Hannah	...	...	...	...	1709-10	74
Seaton, Anna (and 2 children)	...	...	...	1691	78
Skingle, Martha (and child)	...	...	...	1711	88
Smart, Joseph	...	...	...	...	1715	25
Smith, Richard	...	...	...	...	1712	56
Smith, William	...	...	...	...	1721-22	26
Soares, Maria	...	...	...	...	1712	5
Stubs, Anne	...	...	...	...	1701	69
Styleman, Diana	...	...	...	...	1685-86	59
Tainter, Charles	...	...	...	...	1691	63
Torriano, George and Susanna	...	...	...	1741	61
Turner, John	...	...	...	...	1721-22	71
Turton, John	...	...	...	...	1720	40
Unknown (Half Tablet)	...	...	...	...	1684	8
Walsh, Joseph	...	...	...	...	1731	31
Warre, William	...	...	...	...	1715	82
Wendey, Frances	...	...	...	...	1721	30
Wigmore, Thomas	...	...	...	...	1708	60
Williams, Richard	...	...	...	...	1725	21
William, Anthony	...	...	...	...	1691	75
Wrighte, Robert	...	...	...	...	1709	57
Wynch, Sophia (and child)	...	...	...	1754	23
Yale, David	...	...	...	...	1687-88	92

MADRAS: PRINTED BY E. KEYS, AT THE GOVERNMENT PRESS, FORT ST. GEORGE.

View of a part of Fort St. George containing St. Mary's Church
as it appeared after the Siege, 1759.

St. Mary's Church, 1880.

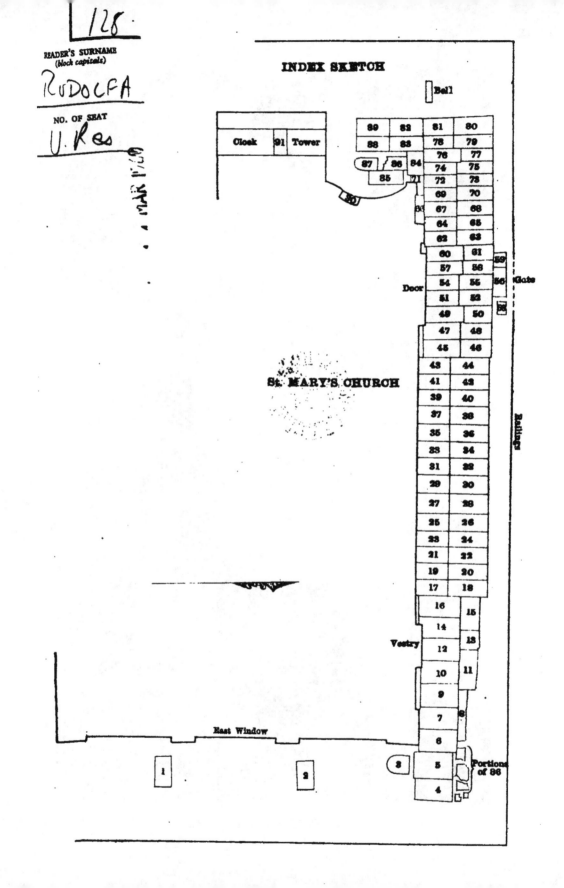

INDEX SKETCH

St. MARY'S CHURCH

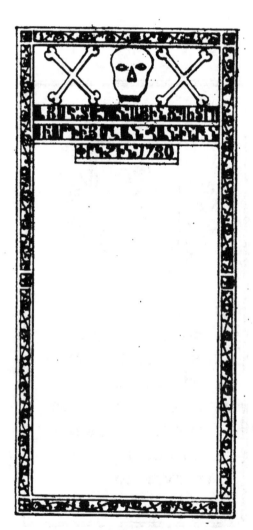

Hic jacet Petrvs
de Torres natio
ne Belga excivita
te Homscot ori
vndvs hic obijt
Avgvsti anno
salvtis 1694 æta
tis svæ 63.
Requiescat in pace.

HERE LYES INTERRED ÿ: BODY
of Mr: Thom: Grajj luner who served
ÿ Rt: Hono Comp: some yeares in qual.
litÿ of one of ÿ: worp: councill in this
place and depared this life Aug: 6:
Anno Domi: 1692: being the 28 yeare
of his Age

Aqui está sepultada
Francisca Melicque filha
de Luis Melicque e de Anto
nia Pestanha Fialha na
tural de Madrastapatam
molher que foj de Dom
Hyeronimo de hita, aqui
faleseo do Segundo par
to de ydade de 17 annos
aos 6 de Janeiro de 1720
REQVIESCAT IN PACE

Aqui Esta Sepultada
Maria Soares de Alvergaria
filha de An.º Soares de
Alverg.ª ede Fran.ºᵈ Ribeira
Natural de Madrasp.ᵗ
Mulher que foi de
Eduard La Cloche
aqual faleceo de jdade
de 40 annos e tres mezes
aos 12 de Janeiro de 1712
equem Ler esta Epitafio
peço p̃ amor de Deos de
rezar p̃ minha alma hũ
Padre nosso ehuã Ave
Maria

AQUI ESTÁ SEPULTADO
O CORPO de NARCIsa
IGNACIA PARAÕ filha
DE IOAÕ PARAÕ Natural
de Madrasta p= Mulher que foi
de FRANCISCO IOZÉ da Silva
A qual faleceo do primeiro parto
De ida da de 18 Annos aos 10 de Dezem
De 1742
Pede pello amor de Deus aos deve, oque Lerem
hũ Padre nossã Chũa Ave Maria p⁰ Sua Alma

Aqui está sepultado o Corpo de
Domingas Ribeira
Legitima filha de
Ant.º Ribr.º e Sebastiana Roiz
e Viuva de Joao Banker
a qual faleceo a os 18 de Setembr
de 1709 Annos: Atatis 69

MENSE MAYO ÆTATIS SVÆ LXXXIII
ALTER VERO ANNO SALVTIS MDCLXXXIV
OCTOBRIS XII ÆTATIS SVÆ LXXXV
TRANSACTIS IN HOC PRÆSIDIOLII
REQVIESCANT IN PACE

HIC IACET

Antonius Coyle de Barnaval
Splendore Natalium in hiber
nia Clarus, Sed Clarioracerrima
Cat. Religronis professione qu
am (Parentum ærumnis, Totiusq
Familiæ bonorum Jacturâ mi
nime attentis) ad extremum Us
que Vitæ servauit iterum (Di
vino favente Numine) divitiis
affluens, pietatis antiquæ non
im remor charitatis. officiis,
aliis Que Virtutibus enituit.
et Sic fortunæ bonis et gratiæ
Cumulatus migravit ad
Dominum
Ætatis Suæ 50, Februarij 6

M. D.C.C. XXV.

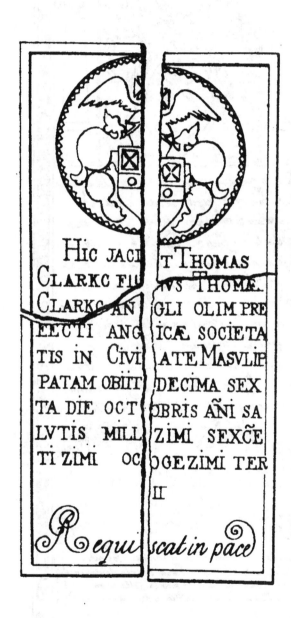

HIC JACET THOMAS
CLARKC FILIVS THOMÆ
CLARKC ANGLI OLIM PRE
EECTI ANGLICÆ SOCIETA
TIS IN CIVITATE MASVLIP
PATAM OBIIT DECIMA SEX
TA DIE OCTOBRIS AÑI SA
LVTIS MILLZIMI SEXCÉ
TIZIMI OCOGEZIMI TER
II

Requiescat in pace

Quæ pauperum Tabernas Regum
Que Turres æquo Pede Pulsat
          Impia Mors
Dilectum hunc Deo & hominibus
Cujus memoria in Benedictione est
          Impie Sustulit
Joannem Scilicet Carvalho Vi
duarum & Orphanorum Deffen
sorem Pauperum Patrem, ami
corum Solatium Familiæ de-
cus... Diem Obiit Supremum
Januarii 13   MDCCXXXIII.

PIO LECTORI

Humana cuncta Fumus Umbra Vanitas
& Scena Imago, & Verbo ut absolvam, nihil
Æternum (Lector) hoc te Alloquor
Æternum ut gaudeam te Apprecare

Panel 1

Silius recondentur Ofsa
IOANNIS GOULDING
Angli apud Londinenses nati
Qui
Artem Arithmeticam
In qua fuit bene versatus
Industria fere singulari
Negotiis Commercialibus
feliciter applicavit
Quem
Dnus Georgius Mortomus Pitt
Hujus Loci Prases
Sagax ille Meriti Indagator
Alti nomine privati Secretarii
Ad se advocavit
Cujus
Scientiam
Diligentiam Integritatem
Officio Machinarum Præfecti
remuneravit

Panel 2

Deinde relinquens
Rerum Administrationem
Domino **Ricardo Benyon**
Successori bene merito
Servum bene merentem
recommendavit
Qui
Summa Cura Labore indefefso
Fiduciam sibi commifsam
prestait
Adeo ut plus aliis
quam sibi viceise
Omnes qui illum noverunt
Confiebuntur
Et rescientibus
Dona Testamentaria
Aque ac manu data
idem testantur
A quibus grati Animi Indicia
plane exhibuit

Panel 3

Quisque Qui
Liberalitatem exercuit
erga Patroni Amico
Pater memoriæ ac erga
Et magnam
Facultatum Parion
Aliis legans
Religionem Dominis pro...
Rex non Dotitarius
Sit Deo Authoribus
redonavit
Confitsuens illos
Testamenti Executore
Et Mandes residuari
Obiis XXVIII Die Junii
Anno Salutis MDCCXXVIII
Anno Ætatis XLII
Cujus Memoriæ
OMP et RB
Hoc Monumentum posuere

Christiane Lector
oculos et pium animum
Huc vertere ne graueris
Defuncte animæ
Maximum facturus leuamen
Maria Henriques quam
Ab Emmanuele Henriques
Et Filippa Botelha progenitam
Dominico q' Mendes coniugatã
Jasananapatà in lucum edidit
lucis usura orbata.
Hoc clauditur Sub marmore
obiit tertio nonas octobris Año Dñi
MDCLXXXIV Ætatis suæ xxxiv

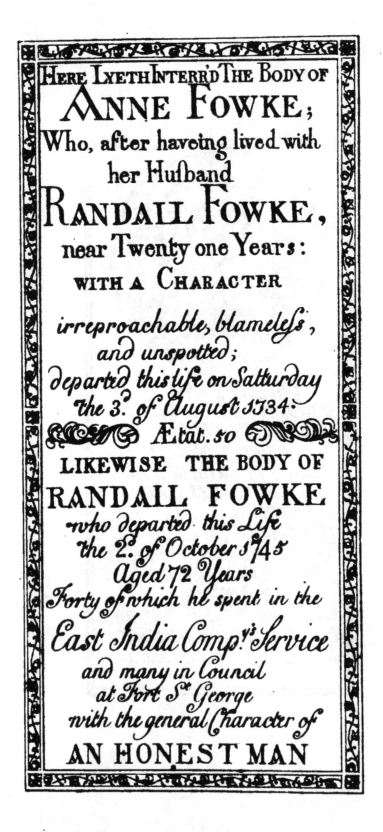

HERE LYETH INTERR'D THE BODY OF

ANNE FOWKE,

Who, after haveing lived with
her Husband

RANDALL FOWKE,

near Twenty one Years:

WITH A CHARACTER

*irreproachable, blameless,
and unspotted;
departed this life on Satturday
the 3.? of August 1734:
Ætat. 50*

LIKEWISE THE BODY OF

RANDALL FOWKE

*who departed this Life
the 2. of October 1745
Aged 72 Years
Forty of which he spent in the*

East India Compᵧˢ Service

*and many in Council
at Fort Sᵗ George
with the general Character of*

AN HONEST MAN

HERE LYETH
Interr'd, the Body of
LUCY, Daughter
of Robert Fleetwood
formerly Chief of
Metchlepatam, and
Wife of Gabriel Poirier
Cap.t Comand.r in Fort
St. George; she depart.
ed this life the 25.th of
October 1732., in the
48.th Year of her Age

Here is also Interr'd the Body of

CAP.t GABRIEL POIRIER
who departed this Life the
4.th day of July 1736
In the 46.th Year of his Age
having Served
the Hon.ble East India Company
upwards of Seventeen Years
in Military Employs

HIC IACET BERNAR
DVS MIDON NATIONE
GERMANVS WITSEN
BOVRGENSIS HAC IN
CIVITATE MADRASPA
TAM MATRIMONIO IVN
CTVS CVM D.Mª. SI
QVEIRA OBIIT IN PACE
OMNIBVS ECCLESIÆ
CATHOLICÆ MVNITVS
SACRAMENTIS DIE XX
VIII DECEBRIS ANI SA
LVTIS MDCLXXXIX.

Orate pro eo.

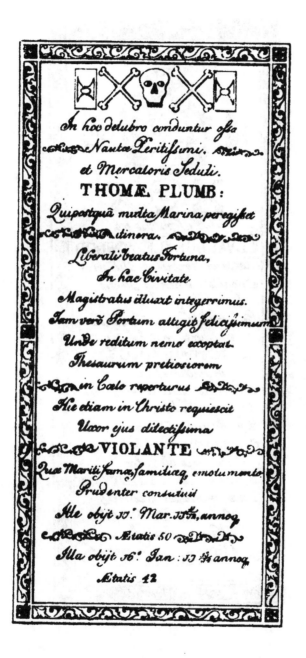

In hoc delubro conduntur ossa
Nautæ Peritissimi,
et Mercatoris Seduli.
THOMÆ PLUMB:
Qui postquam multa Marina peregisset
itinera,
Liberali beatus Fortuna,
In hac Civitate.
Magistratus illuxit integerrimus.
Iam verò Portum attigit felicissimum
Unde reditum nemo exoptat.
Thesaurum pretiosiorem
in Cælo reperturus
Hic etiam in Christo requiescit
Uxor ejus dilectissima
VIOLANTE
Quæ Mariti famæ, familiæq, emolumento,
Prudenter consuluit
Ille obijt 11.° Mar. 15ᵗ.ʰ annoq,
Ætatis 50
Illa obijt 16.° Jan: 11 ᵗʰ annoq,
Ætatis 42

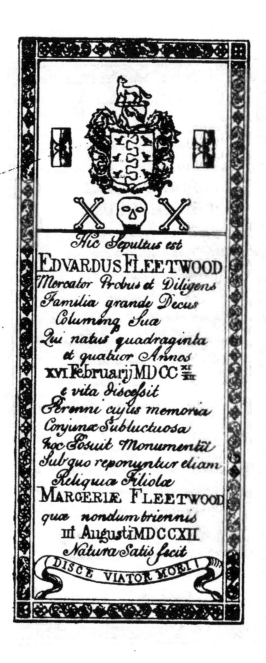

Hic Sepultus est
EDVARDUS FLEETWOOD
Mercator Probus et Diligens
Familia grande Decus
Columing Sua
Qui natus quadraginta
et quatuor Annos
XVI Februarij MDCC XLIII
e vita discessit
Perenni cujus memoria
Conjunx Subluctuosa
hoc Posuit Monumentu
Sub quo reponuntur etiam
Reliquiae Filiolae
MARGERIÆ FLEETWOOD
quæ nondum briennis
III Augusti MDCCXII
Natura Satis fecit
DISCE VIATOR MORI

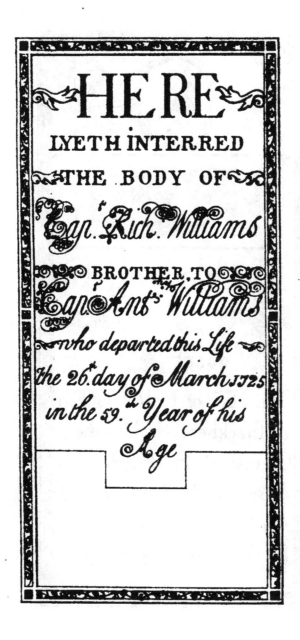

HERE
LYETH INTERRED
THE BODY OF
Capt. Rich. Williams
BROTHER TO
Capt. Antt. Williams
who departed this Life
the 26. day of March 1725
in the 59. Year of his
Age

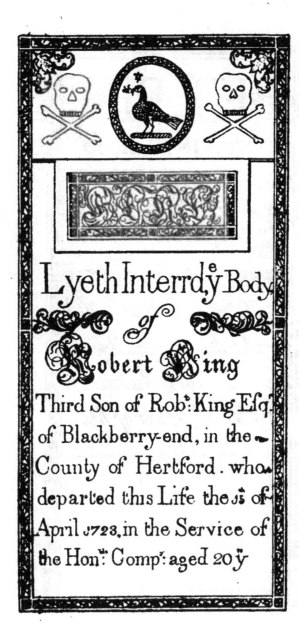

Lyeth Interrd y^e Body,
of
Robert King

Third Son of Rob.: King Esq.
of Blackberry-end, in the
County of Hertford. who
departed this Life the 5: of
April 1723. in the Service of
the Hon.ble Comp.: aged 20 y̋

View of a part of Fort St. George containing St. Mary's Church as it appeared after the Siege 1759

St. Mary's Church, 186_.

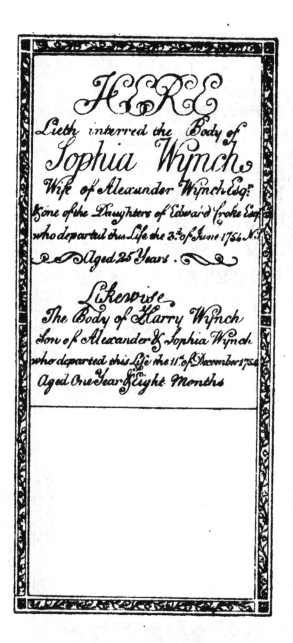

HERE
Lieth interred the Body of
Sophia Wynch
Wife of Alexander Wynch Esq.
one of the Daughters of Edward Croke Esq.
who departed this Life the 3d of June 1754 N.S.
Aged 25 Years.

Likewise
The Body of Harry Wynch
Son of Alexander & Sophia Wynch.
who departed this Life the 11th of December 1754.
Aged One Year & Eight Months

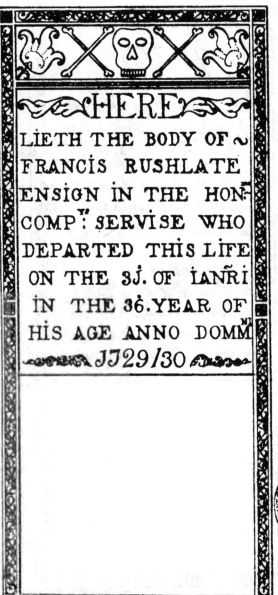

HERE
LIETH THE BODY OF ~
FRANCIS RUSHLATE
ENSIGN IN THE HON^BLE
COMP^Y SERVISE WHO
DEPARTED THIS LIFE
ON THE 3J. OF IANRI
IN THE 36. YEAR OF
HIS AGE ANNO DOMM^NI
J729/30

HERE LYETH INTERR'D
the Body of
IOSEPH SMART Merch.t
who (after having serv'd
the R.t Hon.e Company
in severall Stations
many Years)
departed this life
on the 13th of Decem.br 1715,
being then 5th in Council of
Fort St. George
and Aged about 30 Years.

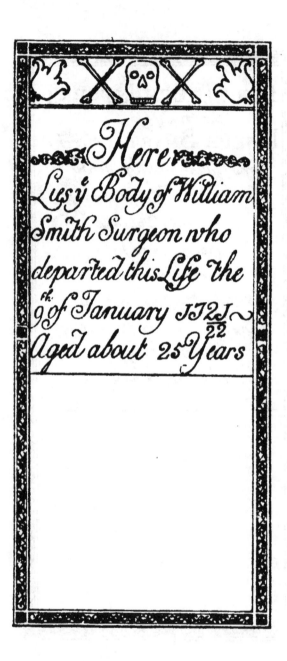

Here
Lies y Body of William
Smith Surgeon who
departed this Life the
9th of January 1721
Aged about 25 Years

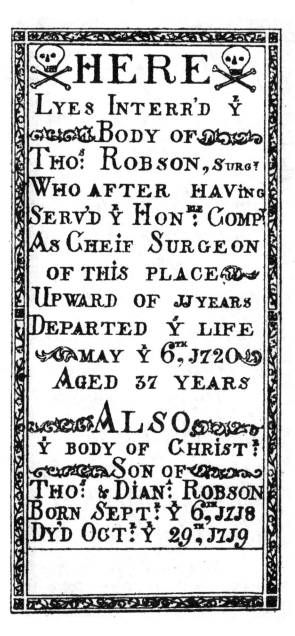

HERE
LYES INTERR'D Ẏ
BODY OF
THO: ROBSON, SURG:
WHO AFTER HAVING
SERV'D Ẏ HON:BLE COMP:
AS CHEIF SURGEON
OF THIS PLACE
UPWARD OF JJ YEARS
DEPARTED Ẏ LIFE
MAY Ẏ 6TH, J720
AGED 37 YEARS

ALSO
Ẏ BODY OF CHRIST:
SON OF
THO: & DIAN: ROBSON
BORN SEPT: Ẏ 6TH, J7J8
DY'D OCT: Ẏ 29TH, J7J9

IN MEMORY
of
Mr Edward Michell
SON
of — Michell of Chittern
in the County of Wilts Esq.
WHO
after having Served the
Hon.th English East Ind.
Company upwards of
nine Years Departed this
Life on the 6th day of June
1745 in the 28th Year of his Age
HIS MONUMENT
is Erected in Compliance
with his Last Will by his
EXECUTORS

HERE LYETH THE BODY OF
HANNAH LEGG
The Wife of IOHN LEGG Esq.

One of the Councill,
and Mayor of this Place
Who, bemoaning the Loss
of his dear and faithfull Spouse
Comforts himself with the hope
that he shall follow her,
to a Happy State:
She dyed in Childbed,
On the 21th. of July 1703;
in the 23d. Year of her Age.

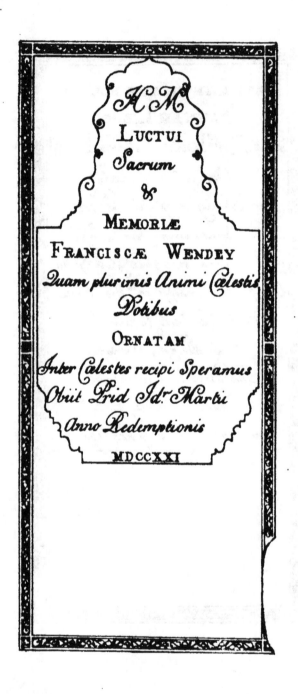

H. M.

Luctui
Sacrum
&

Memoriæ
Franciscæ Wendey
Quam plurimis Animi Cælestis
Dotibus
Ornatam
Inter Cælestes recipi Speramus
Obiit Prid Id.r Martii
Anno Redemptionis
MDCCXXI

In hopes of a Joyfull Resurrection
Here Lyeth the Body of
LUCY. MURIELL.
Wife of M.ʳ Francis Muriell,
Free Merchant of Fort S.ᵗ George
She died July 22.ᵈ 1755.
In the 20.ᵗʰ Year of her Age.

M. S.

CAROLI HOPKINS

Qui vita defunctus est

V.° die Martis MDCCXI

Anno Ætatis LIII.tio

Filii pietas

Posuit

MDCCXXXIX

HERE

LYETH THE BODY

OF

Capt. Tho. Aubone

Commr of ye James & Mary
who departed this Life
the 19th day of Augt 1725.
in the 49th Year of his Age

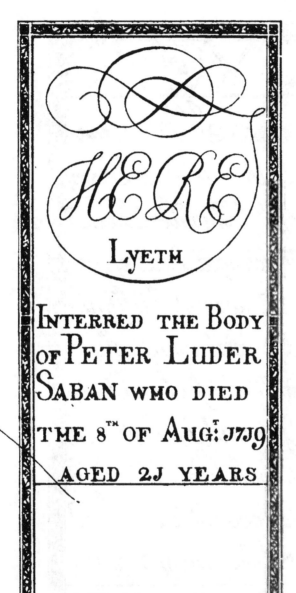

HERE LYETH INTERRED THE BODY OF PETER LUDER SABAN WHO DIED THE 8ᵀᴴ OF AUG:ᵀ 1719 AGED 21 YEARS

Here

Lieth inter'd the Body
of John Maubert Diamond
Merch.^t aged about 33 Years
and departed this Life the
15 of October 1724 he liv'd
in Madrass about Eleven
Years with a perfect
Reputation and design'd
to England had he liv'd
till January 172 ½

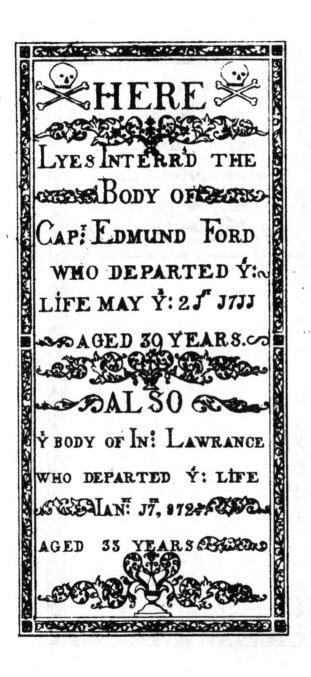

HERE

LYES INTERR'D THE
BODY OF
CAP: EDMUND FORD
WHO DEPARTED Y:
LIFE MAY Y: 25 1711
AGED 39 YEARS.

ALSO

Y BODY OF IN: LAWRANCE
WHO DEPARTED Y: LIFE
IAN: 17, 1724
AGED 33 YEARS

HERE LYETH INTERR'D,
the Body of
IOHN FULLAGAR;
who departed this Life
May the 30th 1727
In the 27th Year of his Age

HERE LYETH INTERRD,
the Body of
ELIZABETH JENNINGS
Wife of
William Jennings Esqr
Second in Council of this Place,
who Dyed in Child-bed
the 7th day of Feb.y 1755,
In the 30th Year of her Age
Haveing left Issue
One Son by her former husband
Mr Robert Wrighte;
and two Sons & two Daughters
by said William Jennings Esqr.

HERE LYETH INTEBR'D,
the Body of
IOHN TURTON,
Who after having Served
the Hon.ble Company for the
Space of Nine Years,
was at length preferr'd to be
Youngest of Council in this
Place; in which Station he
departed this Life
on the 25th day of April
Anno Domini 1720.
Aged about 27 Years.

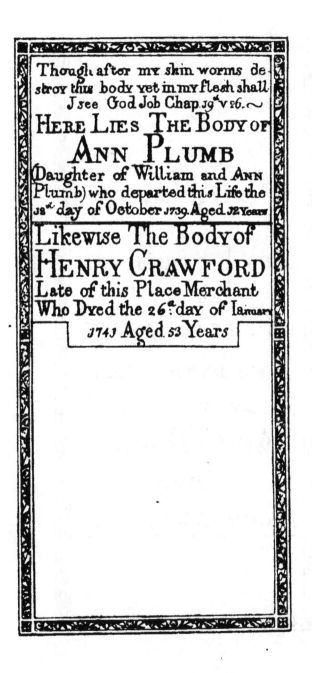

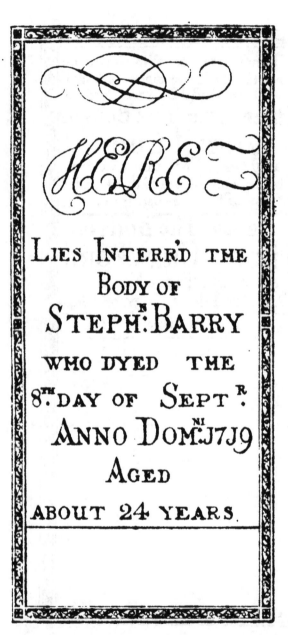

HERE

LIES INTERR'D THE
BODY OF
STEPH^N: BARRY
WHO DYED   THE
8TH DAY OF   SEPT^R.
ANNO DOM^{NI}: J7J9
AGED
ABOUT 24 YEARS.

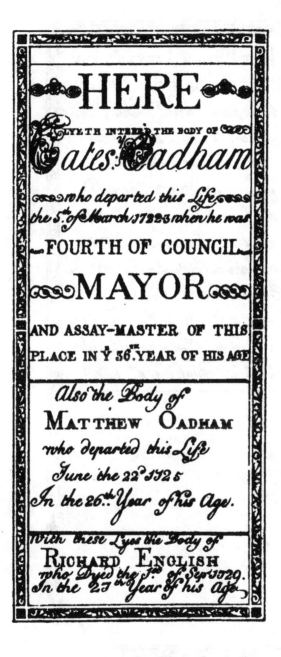

HERE

LYETH INTER'D THE BODY OF

Gates Oadham

*who departed this Life
the 5.th of March 1722-3 when he was*

FOURTH OF COUNCIL

MAYOR

AND ASSAY-MASTER OF THIS

PLACE IN Y 56.th YEAR OF HIS AGE

Also the Body of
MATTHEW OADHAM
*who departed this Life
June the 22.d 1725
In the 26.th Year of his Age.*

With these Lyes the Body of
RICHARD ENGLISH
*who Dyed the 3.d of Sep.r 1729.
In the 23.th Year of his Age*

HERE LYETH INTERR'D, THE
BODY OF SAMUEL BROWN,
who departed this Life July 5. 1695
together with his Father and Mother
SAMUEL BROWN, and ANN ;
afterwards FOQUET deceased;
the former, December 23: 1698;
the Latter, September 1: 1715,
with them Lyeth also Interr'd the
Body of CHARLES, Son of
CHARLES LONG by ELIZABETH
his Wife, their Sister and Daughter.
he Dyed June the 5.th 1720.

S^A
DE FRANCYSCO
MARQVESQVE
FALESEOEM 23 DE
AGOSTO J687

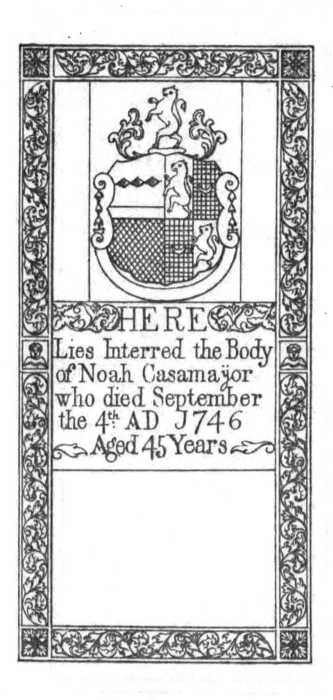

HERE
Lies Interred the Body
of Noah Casamajor
who died September
the 4th AD 1746
Aged 45 Years

Here Lies interred the body of
John Barker
who departed y^e life y^e 4th of Decem^r
1707
Also y^e bodys of Robt Mary, Fran^s
John, Fran. Timothy, Nathan^l
Anne & Benjamin his Children,
Likewise y^e bodys of Jno & Fran^s
his Grand Children.

HER
Lyes interred y' Body of M:
Peter Large Merch: who ha
ving liv'd 39 Years in India
Departed this Life March
29. 1694: in the 78: Year
of his Age

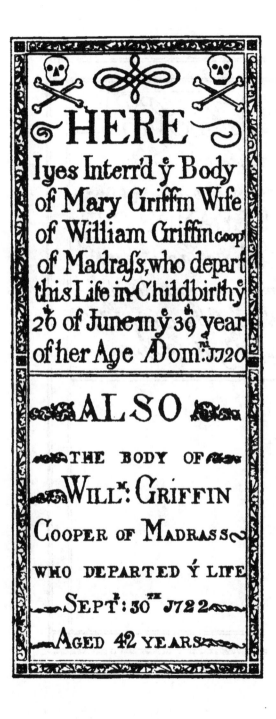

HERE
Iyes Interr'd ý Body
of Mary Griffin Wife
of William Griffin coop
of Madraſs, who depart
this Life in Childbirth ý
26 of June in ý 39 year
of her Age A Dom: 1720

ALSO

THE BODY OF

WILL: GRIFFIN

COOPER OF MADRASS

WHO DEPARTED Ý LIFE

SEPT: 30 1722

AGED 42 YEARS

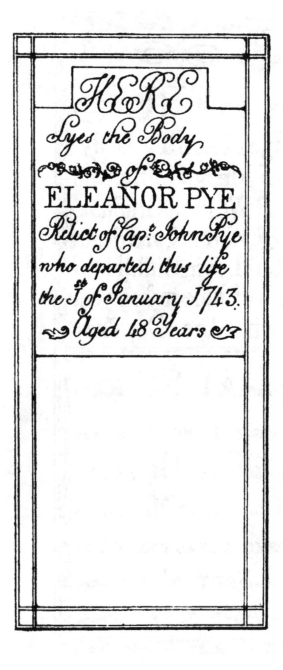

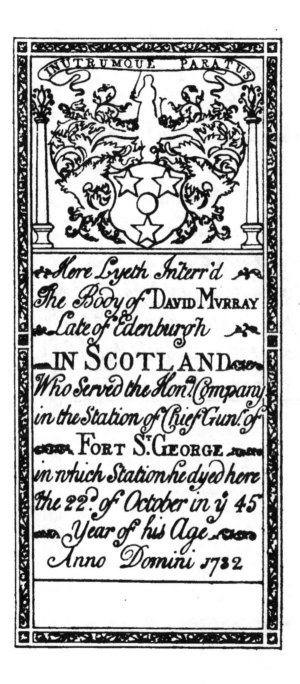

IN UTRUMQUE PARATUS

Here Lyeth Interr'd
The Body of DAVID MVRRAY
Late of Edenburgh
IN SCOTLAND
Who Served the Honᵇˡᵉ Company
in the Station of Chief Gunᵉʳ of
FORT Sᵗ. GEORGE
in which Station he dyed here
the 22ᵈ of October in ẙ 45
Year of his Age
Anno Domini 1732

UNDER THIS STONE
Lyeth the Body of
Capt. ALEXANDER FULLERTON,
Born in Argyleshire,
North Brittain,
Anno Dom. 1653
And serv'd the East India
Company, as Capt. of a Comp. of
Foot Soldiers, from the Year
1709, till he departed this Life
March, 10th A.D. 1723

The house   all living

appointed for

There the wicked cease from troubling
and there the weary be at rest.
There the prisoners rest together,
they hear not the voice of the oppressor.
The small and great are there, and
the servant free from his master.
Job 3. 1718, 19.

HERE LYETH INTERR'D
the Body of
RICHARDS HIGGINSON
Son of
Nathan. Higginson Esq.r
formerly
Govern.d of Fort St. George.
He Dyed the 7.th of June 1726,
In the 32. Year of his Age:
being then 5.th in Council.
He was a Man greatly
Esteem'd for his Integrity.

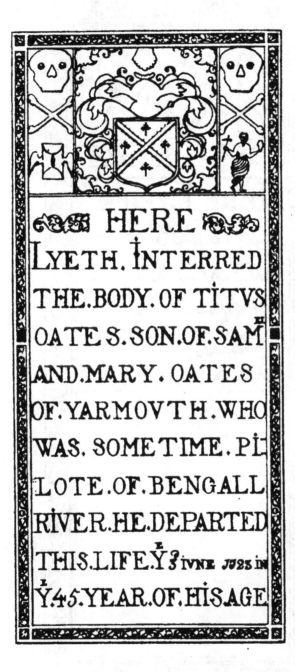

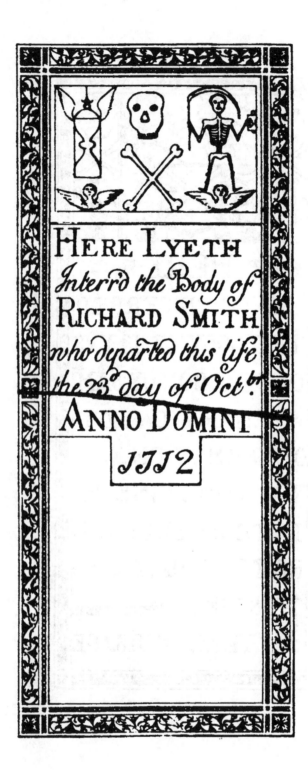

HERE LYETH
Interr'd the Body of
RICHARD SMITH
who departed this life
the 23ᵈ day of Octᵇʳ
ANNO DOMINI
1712

Here Lyeth Interr'd
Mr. Robt. Wrighte
Merchant,
Third Son of
Sr Nathl. Wrighte Knt.
Sometime Lord Keeper
of the Great Seal to his
late Majesty William
the Third, and to her present Majesty Anne
Queen of Great Brittain
&c. who departed this
life the 16th day of Octr.
1709

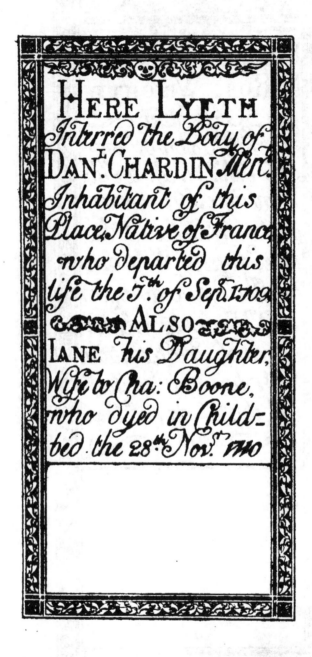

Here Lyeth
Interred the Body of
Danᴵ. Chardin Merᵗ
Inhabitant of this
Place, Native of France,
who departed this
life the 5ᵗʰ of Sepᵗ 1709,
ALSO
Iane his Daughter,
Wife to Cha: Boone,
who dyed in Child-
bed the 28ᵗʰ Novᵗ 1710

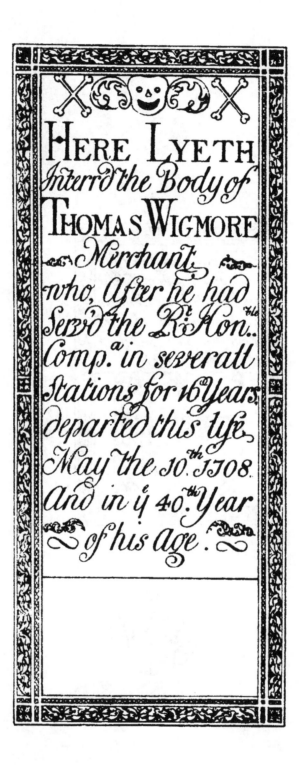

HERE LYETH
Interr'd the Body of
THOMAS WIGMORE
Merchant
who, After he had
Serv'd the Rt Hon.ble
Comp.a in severall
Stations for 16 Years.
departed this life
May the 10.th 1708.
And in ij 40.th Year
of his Age.

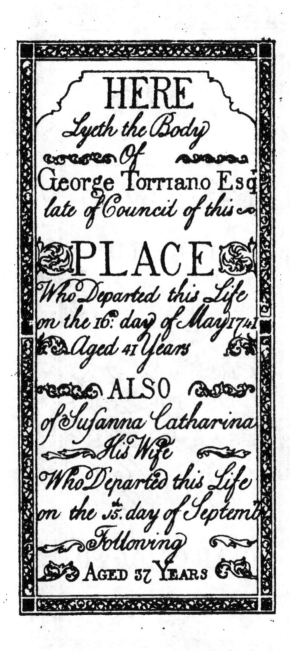

HERE
Lyeth the Body
Of
George Torriano Esq
late of Council of this
PLACE
Who Departed this Life
on the 16: day of May 1741
Aged 41 Years

ALSO
of Susanna Catharina
His Wife
Who Departed this Life
on the 15. day of Septemb
Following
AGED 37 YEARS

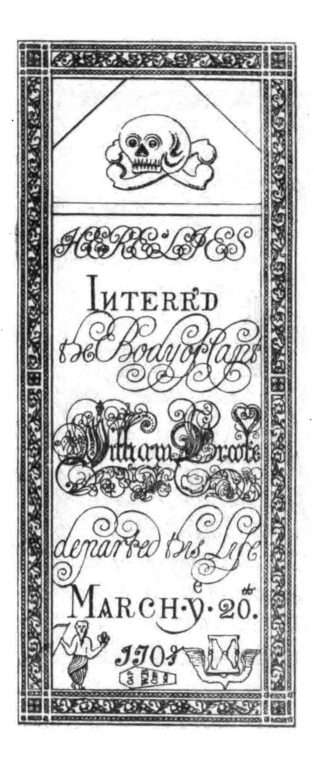

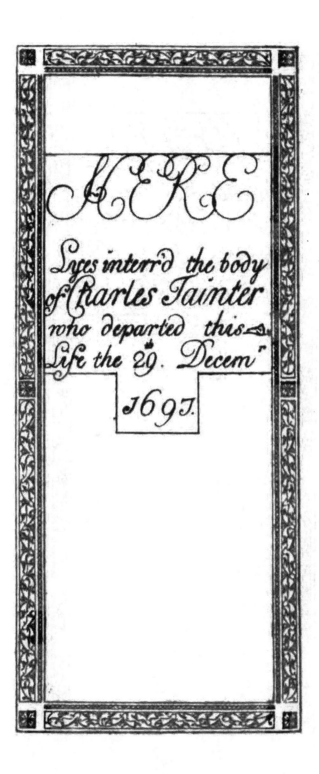

HERE Lyes interr'd the body of Charles Tainter who departed this Life the 29 Decemr 1697.

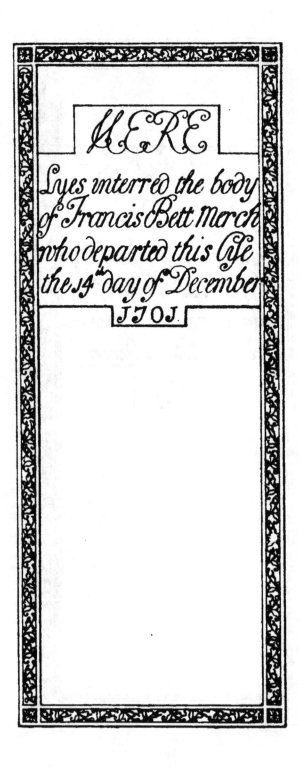

HERE
Lyes interred the body
of Francis Bett Merch
who departed this life
the 14th day of December
1701

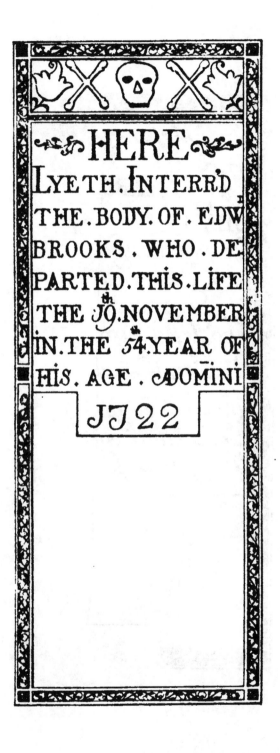

In Memory
IOHN & DEB{RAH} BRABO
Son and Daugh
IOHN BRABOUR
Deceased;
Who Dyed Infa
DEB{RAH} on y 15 May
& IOHN on y 18 May
Both in the Fou
Year of their A

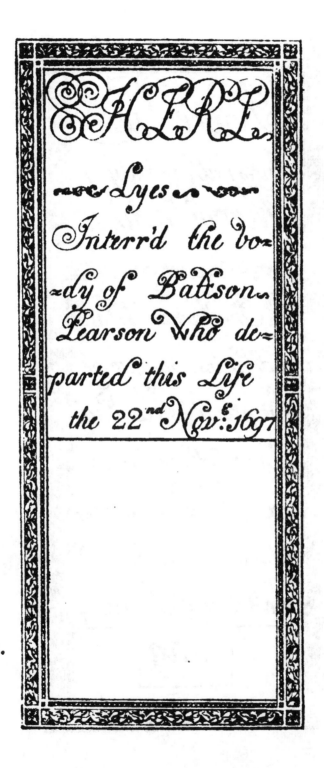

HERE Lyes Interr'd the body of Battson Pearson who departed this Life the 22nd Novr. 1697

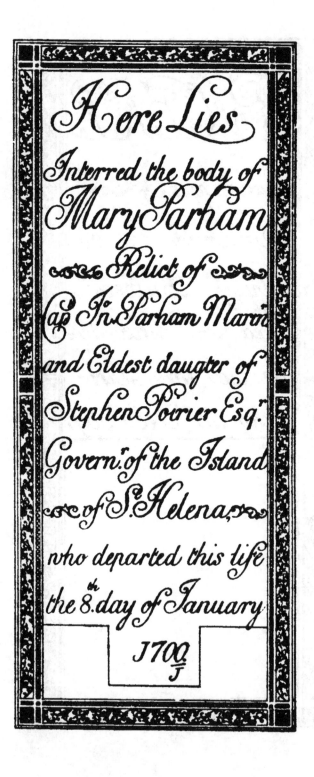

Here Lies

Interred the body of
Mary Parham
Relict of
Cap. Jn. Parham Marin
and Eldest daugter of
Stephen Poirier Esqr.
Govern. of the Island
of St. Helena,
who departed this life
the 8. day of January
1700/1

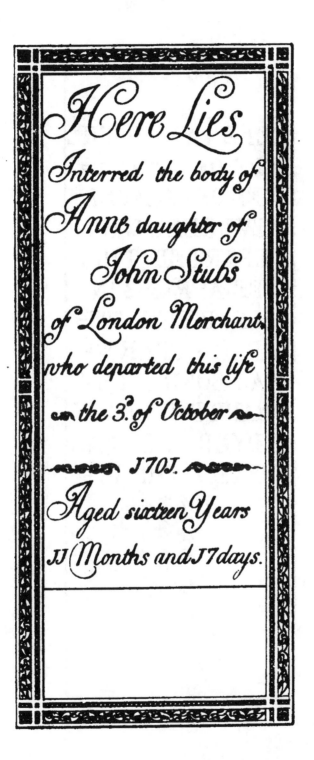

HERE LYETH THE
BODY OF ANN ≈
WIFE OF SAMVEL
MEVERELL WHO
DEPARTED THIS
LIFE APRIL 18 IN
CHILD BIRTH WITH
A DAUGHTER W^{ch}≈
WAS BORNE THE
8th BAPTIZED MARY
12 DYED AND WAS
BURYED THE 13 ≈
1689·/

Here
Lies the Bo[dy]
John Turr[ell]
Son of Nat[haniel]
& Elizab: [Turrell]
Born the 13 day of
March 17½ and
departed ỹ Life the
same day

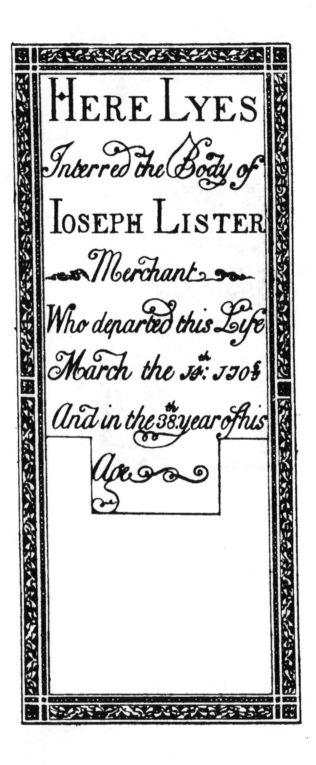

HERE LYES

Interred the Body of
FRANCIS ELLIS Esq.
Who after he had serv'd
the R.ble Hon.ble Comp.a.
for many Years here
& in Bengall dyed
Second of Councill
in this Place March
the 6. 170 4/5

Heart, Vertue, Grace, centerd
  in one
Adorn'd y dust that lyes
  below this Stone,
Now, who has strength
  t'oppose y Almighty's had
None can against his
  deadly terrors stand,
At length the Archer
  grim his Arrow shott
He seis'd from her w. she
  from God had gott,
Such moves our minds
  his greatness to adore,
Even love his goodness &
  revere his pow'r
Above, her Soul-w. raptu
  :rous joys ascends
To God, in Heaven her life
  with praises ends
On high w. God, this hea
  venly Soul remains,
No return thence till all is in
  ⁓ to Flames ⁓
Hannah Seaton Wife of
Cap. Frant. Seaton dyed 1. Febru.
  ætat. 37

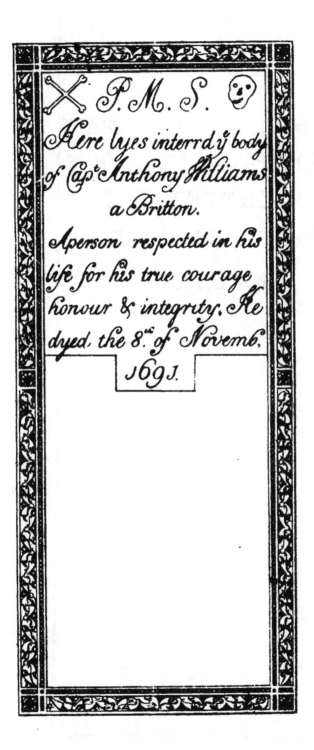

P. M. S.

Here lyes interrd ÿ body
of Cap.ᵗ Anthony Williams
a Britton.

A person respected in his
life for his true courage
honour & integrity. He
dyed the 8.ᵗʰ of Novemb,
1691.

HERE LIETH IOHN CORNISH W
HO DEPARTED THIS LIFE T
H EXII DAY OF MARCH IN
T HE YEARE OF OILR LO
RD COD J664

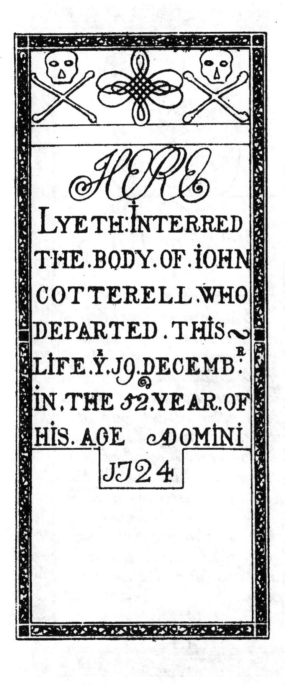

HERE
LYE TH: INTERRED
THE . BODY . OF . IOHN
COTTERELL . WHO
DEPARTED . THIS
LIFE . Ẏ . 19 . DECEMB.ᴿ
IN . THE 52 . YEAR . OF
HIS . AGE ᴀDOMINI
1724

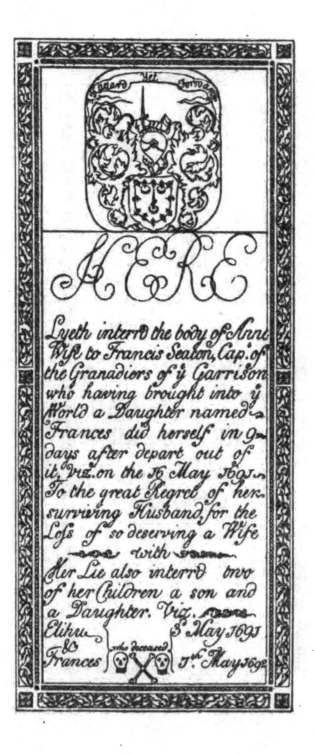

HIC JACET

Thomæ Marshall
Uxor Dilectissima.

Quæ Mortem Obijt
Decimo Octavo die May 1701
Annoq Ætatis decimo octavo

HERE LYETH
Interr'd the Body of
ROBERT ATKINSON
who after haveing
serv'd many Years
Gunner of this Garri-
son departed this
life the 27th Aug. 1711
in y 47th Year of his Age

Here also is Interred
the Body of
CHARs ATKINSON his Son
who died on y 22d day
of December 1734.
Aged about Seventeen Years

HERE LIE

The Mortall remaines of
Jane Keaton,
Once the pious & beloved wife
of
Cap Samuel Keaton,
who dyed in child birth
the 25.º of April An. Dom. 1703
Annoq, ætatis 21
Favor is deceitful, & beauty
is vain, but a woman y. feareth
the Lord, she shall be praised.
Proverbs 31. 30.

HERE ALSO LYETH
Interr'd the Body of
Cap.ᵗ Sam.ᵗ Keaton,
who departed this life
the 25.º day of Dec.ᵇ 1708
and in y 38. Year of his age

Hic Jacet
OULIELMUS WARRE ARMIG
qui, sub Honorabili
Anglorum Societate,
Varijs functus Officijs,
Madraßpatnæ tandem
Tertius a Consilijs,
Mortem oppetiit
VI: MAII MDCCXV.
Natus circiter XXXV Annos

Here Lyeth
WILLIAM WARRE ESQ:
who haveing serv'd
the Honourable Company
in severall Stations.
Dyed (while he was
Third of Council
in Fort S: George)
on the 6th of May 1715,
Aged about 35 Years.

HERE LYETH INTERR'D
the Body of
CAROLINA BURNISTON
Relictof
John Burniston Esq. dec;
Sometime Depty Govr of ye
Island Bombay,
who departed this life the
11th day of July 1708,
ALSO
Two of her Grandsons Viz.
JOHN
Son of Will: Aislabie Esqr
Generall of India, and
JOHN
Son of John Scattergood
of this Place Mercht:
who both dyed Infants.

HERE LYETH
Interr'd the Body of
THOMAS Son of
CHRISTOPHER and
FLORENTIA CRADOCK
Who departed this life
on the 13th August 1712
In the 4th Year of his Age

HERE LYETH THE BODY OF
NATHANIEL FOXCROFT SON OF
GEORGE FOXCROFT AGENT AND
GOVERNOR IN FORT ST. GEORGE
HE WAS BORNE INTO THIS WORLD
THE 6TH OF SEPTEMBER 1635 AND
TRANSLATED INTO A BETTER TO
THE RESVRRECTION OF THE
JVST THE 26 OF OCTOBER 1670
AFTER HE HAD FINISHED HIS
PILGRIMAGE ON THE EARTH 35
YEARES HAVEING ALWAIES
EXHIBITED ALL THE HONOR DUE
FROM A DEAR AND DVTIFULL
SON TO HIS PARENTS AND BY
HIS UNIVERSAL OBLIGING &
INGENIOUS CONVERSATION
OBTAINED A GOOD REPORT &
LEFT A GOOD NAME WITH
ALL MEN

A good name is better than a precious
oyntment and the day of death then
the day of ones birth Eccle 7.1.
The memory of y just is blessed Psa xi.7
The righteous shall be in everlasting
remembrance Psa 112.6

MEMORIÆ SACRVM
DOMINÆ ELIZABETH BAKER
DOMINI AARONIS BAKER
(ANGLORVM HISCE LOCIS
NEGOTIANTIVM PRÆSID)
VXORIS DILECTISSIMÆ
QVÆ,
MARITO AD INDOS   CANTI,
RELICTO SOLO P
SESE IVNGEBAT   M
ILLVMQVE
PROXIME PROMON   R
BONÆ SPEI, SPEI   IM
MARINO PARTV BEABAT
SED TANDEM
POST LONGAS PELAGI MINAS,
INSALVBREMQVE IAVÆ AEREM
QVÆ LIBENS VNA PASSA EST,
TRISTISSIMVM PRO COELIS
(PRO QVIBVS SOLIS VOLVIT)
MORIENS RELINQVEBAT
AVGVSTI: 5.ANº.1652.

HERE
Lyes Interred y̌. Bodij of Richard
Browne Esq; who Served y̌. Rᵗ
Hon͘ᵇᵗᵉ Comp͘ᵃ: many yeares Cheif ꝟ
Their affaires in Vizagapatnam and
Departed This Life the 26ᵗʰ of January
Anno Domini 169¾

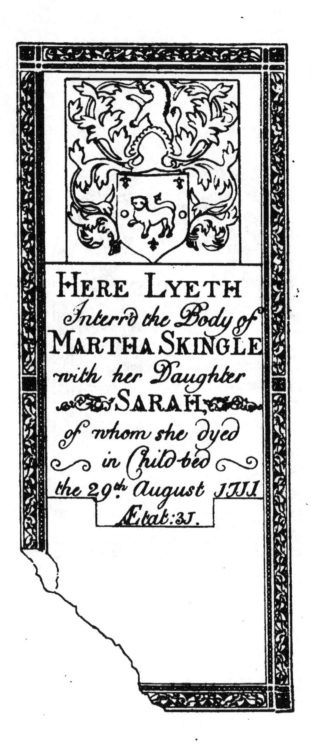

HERE LYETH
Interr'd the Body of
MARTHA SKINGLE
with her Daughter
SARAH,
of whom she dyed
in Child-bed
the 29th August 1711
Ætat: 31.

HERE LYETH INTERR'D
the Body of
Mr FRANCᶜ COOKE
MERCHANT,
who after having
serv'd the Rᵗ Honᵇˡᵉ...
Compᵃ in the Station
of Assaymaster yᵉ
space of 12 Years;
departed this life
the 3ᵈ of Febᵧ 1703/4
in the 39ᵗʰ Year of his
Age.

VIATOR

Quicunque es Sifte
Sifte inquam paululum nec fruftra
Si saltem Christianus es
Moræ pretium erit
Nec non lachryma
Cum iacere hic fcias
HENRICVM GREENHILL
Splendidæ suæ Familiæ
Splendorem Maximum
&
Honorabilis Mercatorū Anglorū Societatis
diam Orientalē negotiantium
Agentem Vnum
Et Nemini Secur lum
Cumper Deocr
Summa cum fedulitate
Et fpectata probitate
Functus eft Officio fuo
Functus eft
Anno
CHRISTI MDCLVIII
Ætatis fuæ XLV
. . . . f non nen
impertire
Et Abi

M S

FRAN: HASTINGS

HERE
Lyes interred the body of Joseph
Hummers who served the R.t Hon.ble
English East India Comp.a several
Years, as 2.d m Council of Fort S.t
George; in 10.th station he departed
this Life: on the 28.th of May 1680.

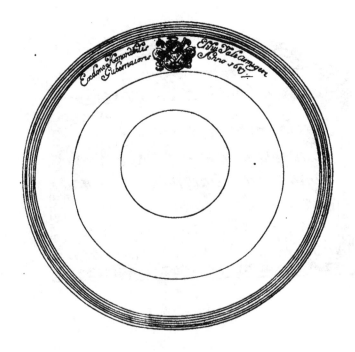

Exdono Honoraliss [68] Dominæ quæ excessil exhac Vila
Dom [68] Mariæ Goldsborough (1698) 30 Die Nouembris 1698

Endono Honoralias⁰ Dominos quos excessit exhac Vita
Dom⁰ Mariæ Goldsborough (1699) 30 Die Nouembris 1698

A

Circumſpection in their ſeveral Stations, That we may all Diſcharg our reſpective Duties faithfully, and Live virtuouſly in due Obedience to our Superiors, and in Love, Peace, and Charity one toward another, That theſe *Indian* Nations among whom we dwell, ſeeing our ſober and righteous Converſation, may be induced to have a juſt Eſteem for our Holy Profeſſion of the Goſpel of our Lord and Saviour Jeſus Chriſt, to whom be Honour, Praiſe, and Glory, now a i ſr Ever. *Amen.*

Imprimatur
April 20, 1694.

H. LONDON

CPSIA information can be obtained
at www.ICGtesting.com
Printed in the USA
BVHW071838161219
566813BV00016B/1268/P

9 781164 642213